THIS BOOK BELONGS TO

Apple

Dot me

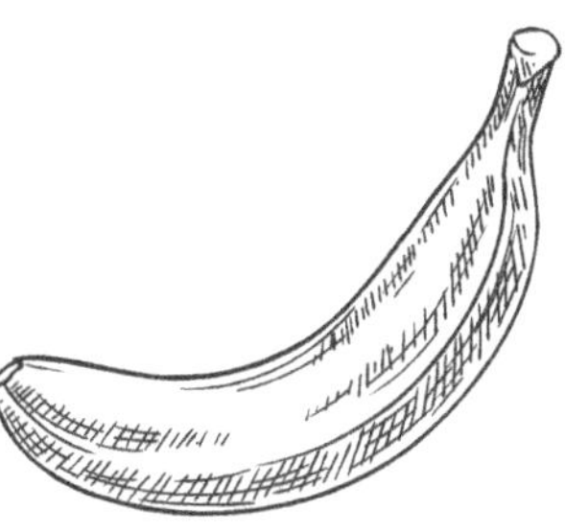

Banana

Dot me

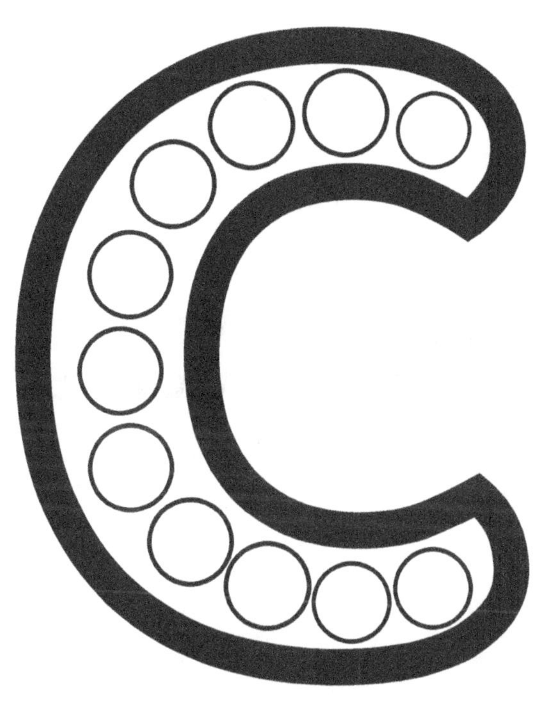

Car

Dot me

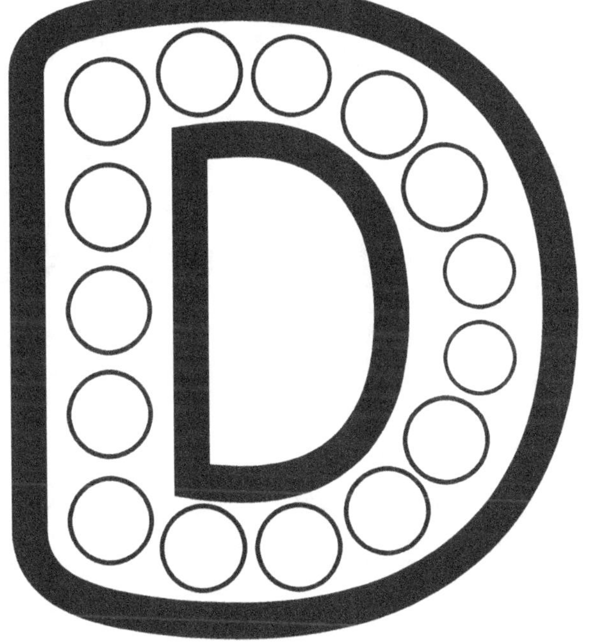

Door

Dot me

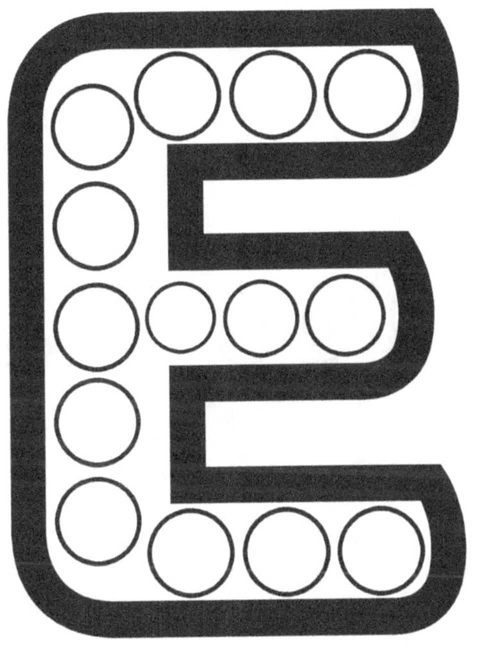

Egg

Dot me

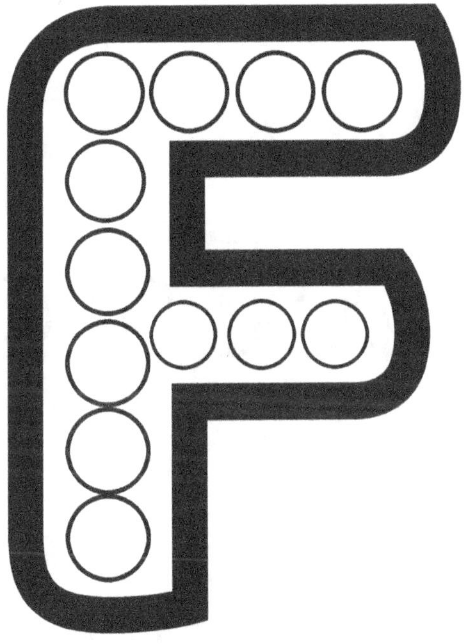

Fruit

Dot me

Gift

Dot me

House

Dot me

Ice Cream

Dot me

Jug

Dot me

Kite

Dot me

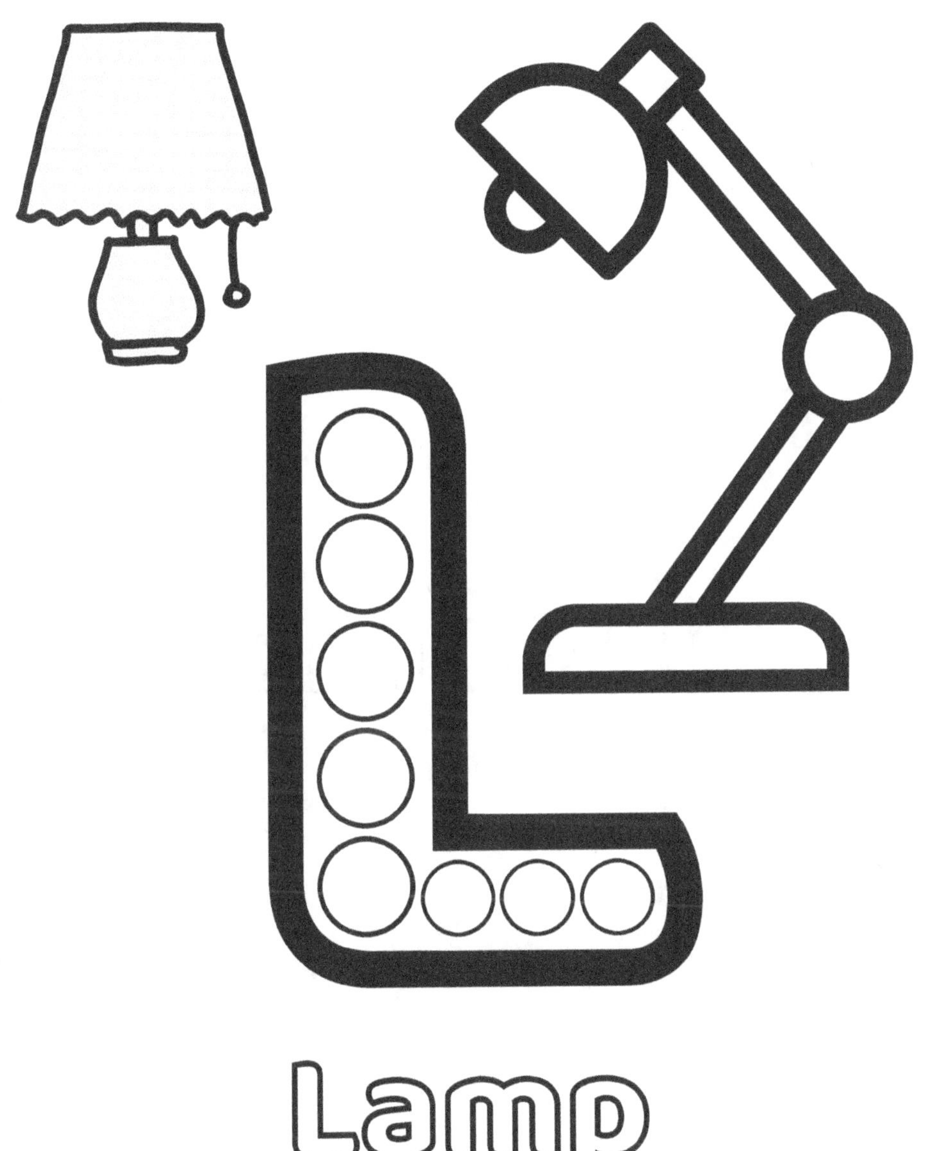

Lamp

Dot me

Mango

Dot me

Nest

Dot me

Orange

Dot me

Pen

Dot me

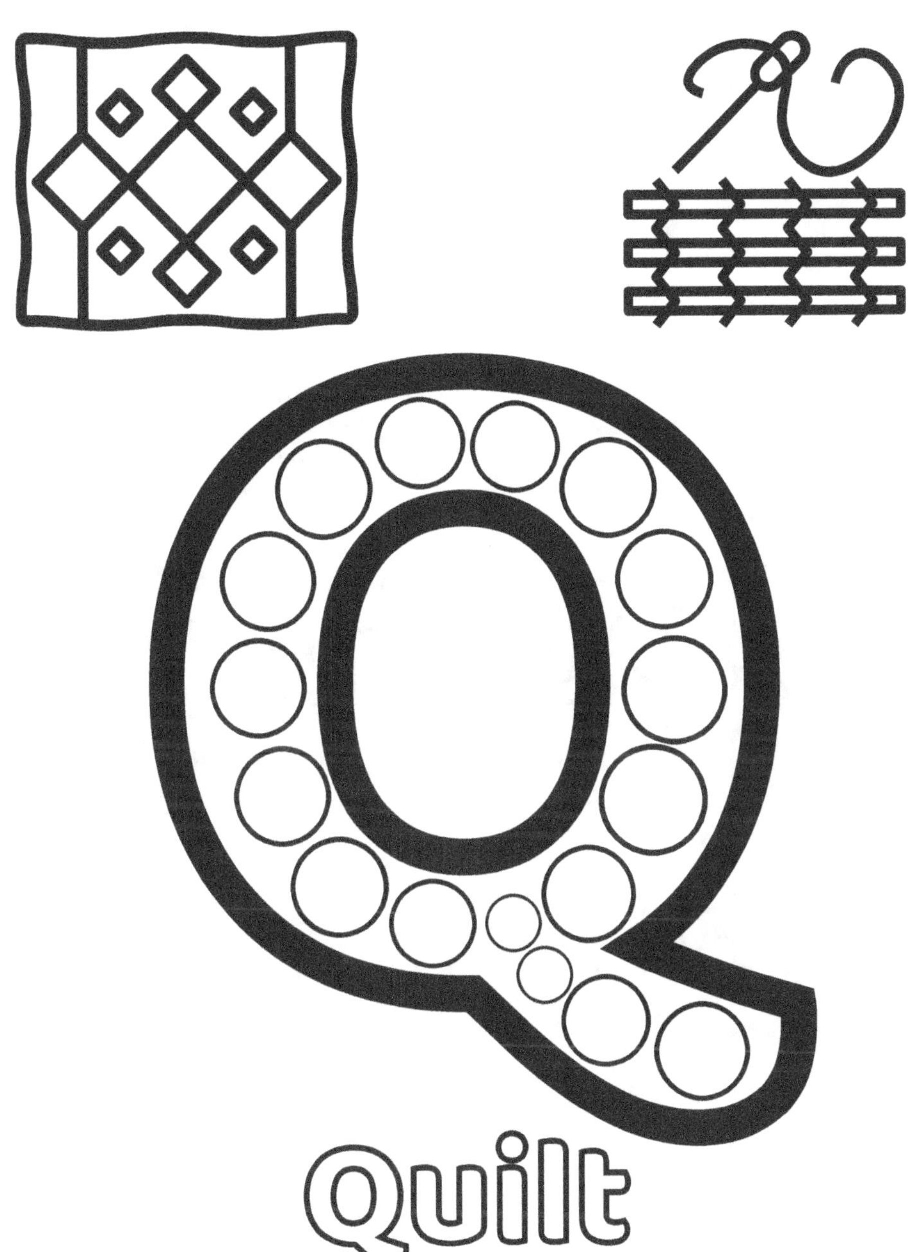
Quilt

Dot me

Rose

Dot me

Sun

Dot me

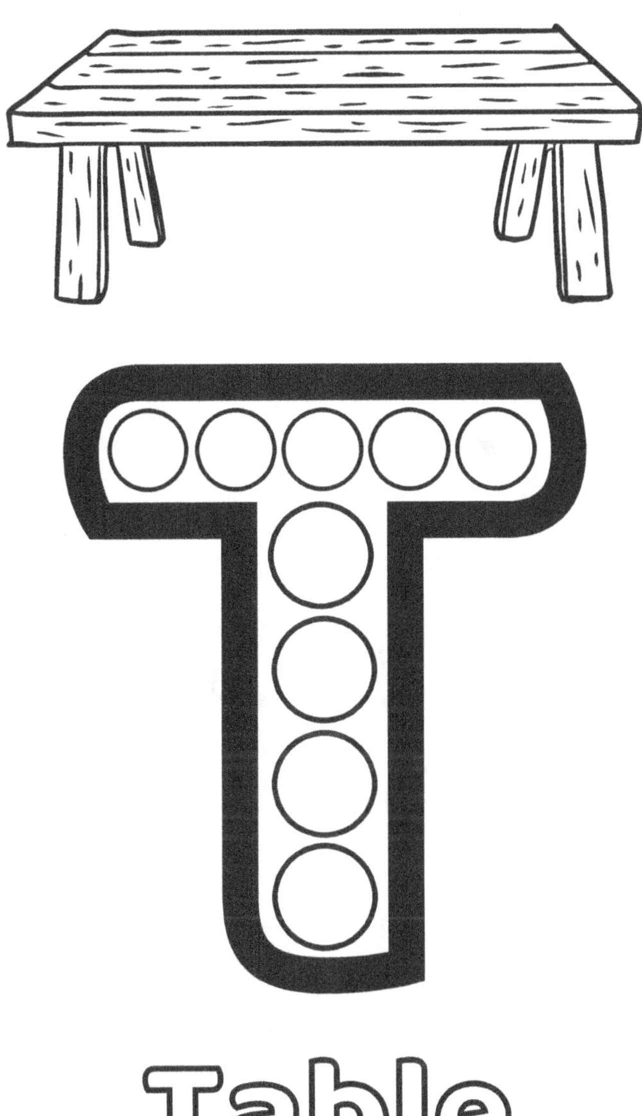

Table

Dot me

Umbrella

Dot me

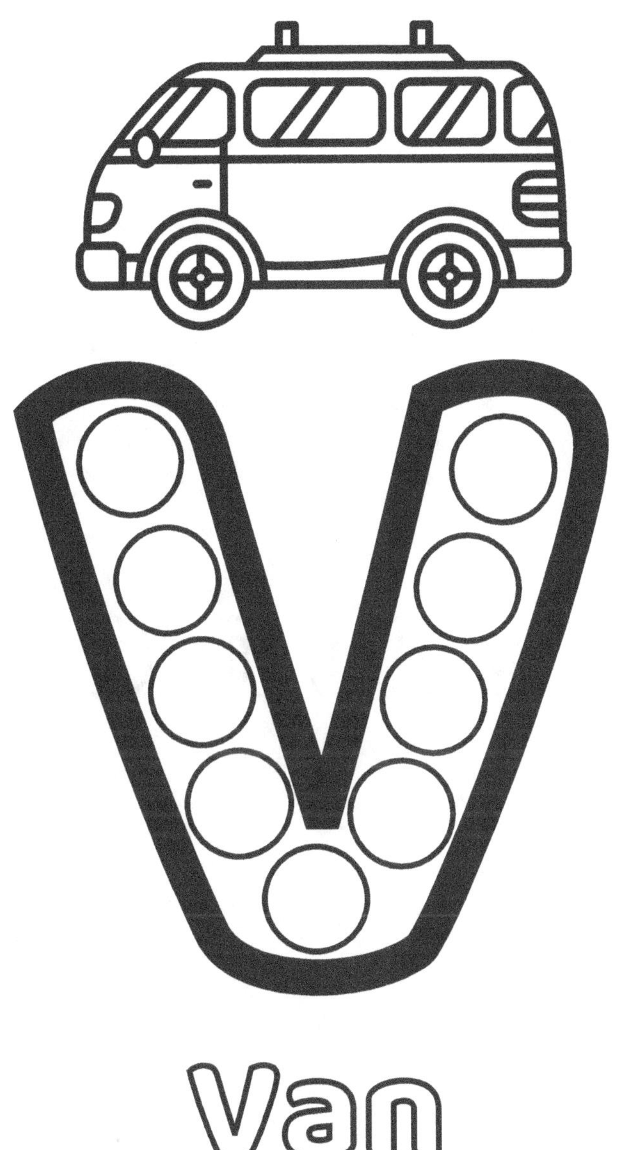

Van

Dot me

Watch

Dot me

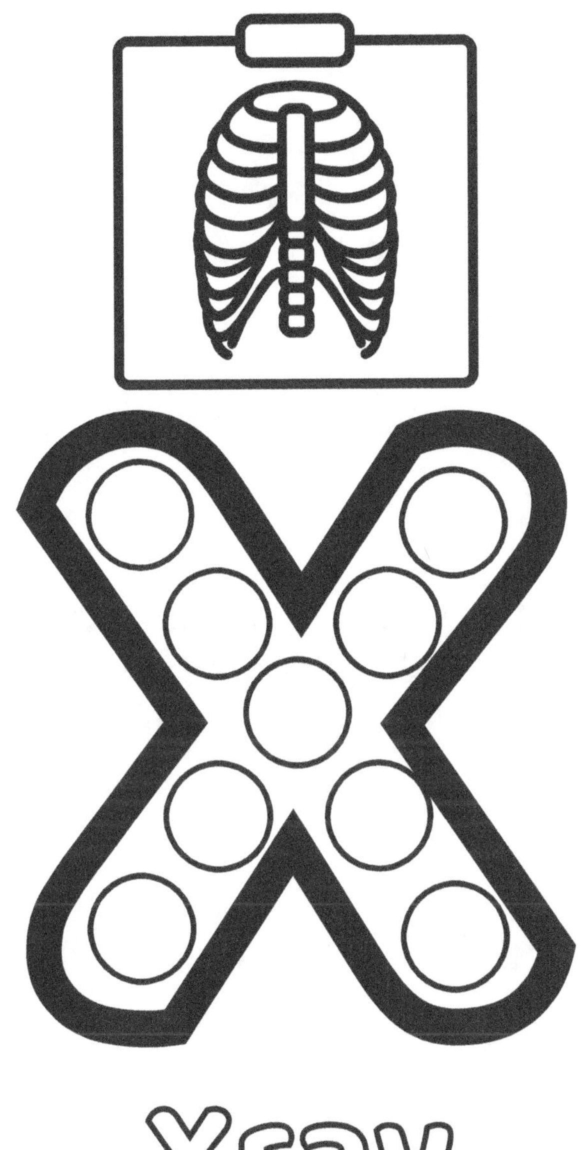

Xray

Dot me

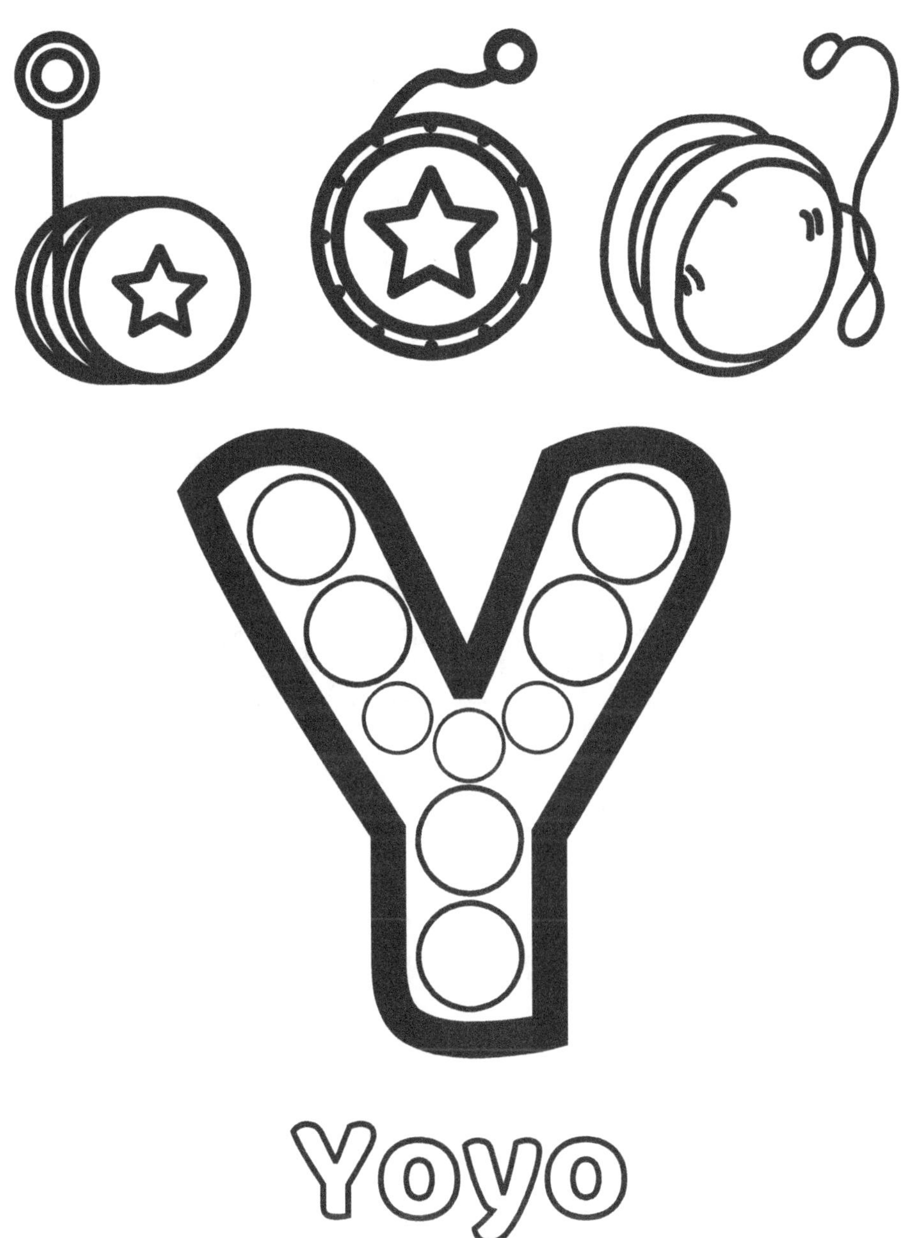

Yoyo

Dot me

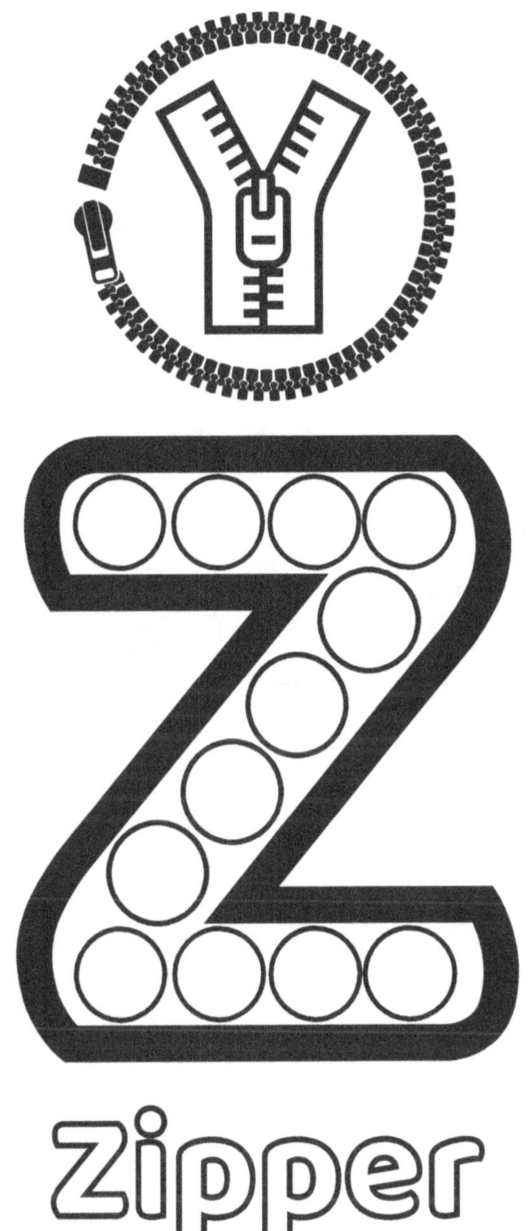

Zipper

Dot me